CRETACEOUS

120   110   100   90   80   70   60   50   40

SAURUS"   ARGENTINOSAURUS
                          ANTARCTOSAURUS

ntinosaurus

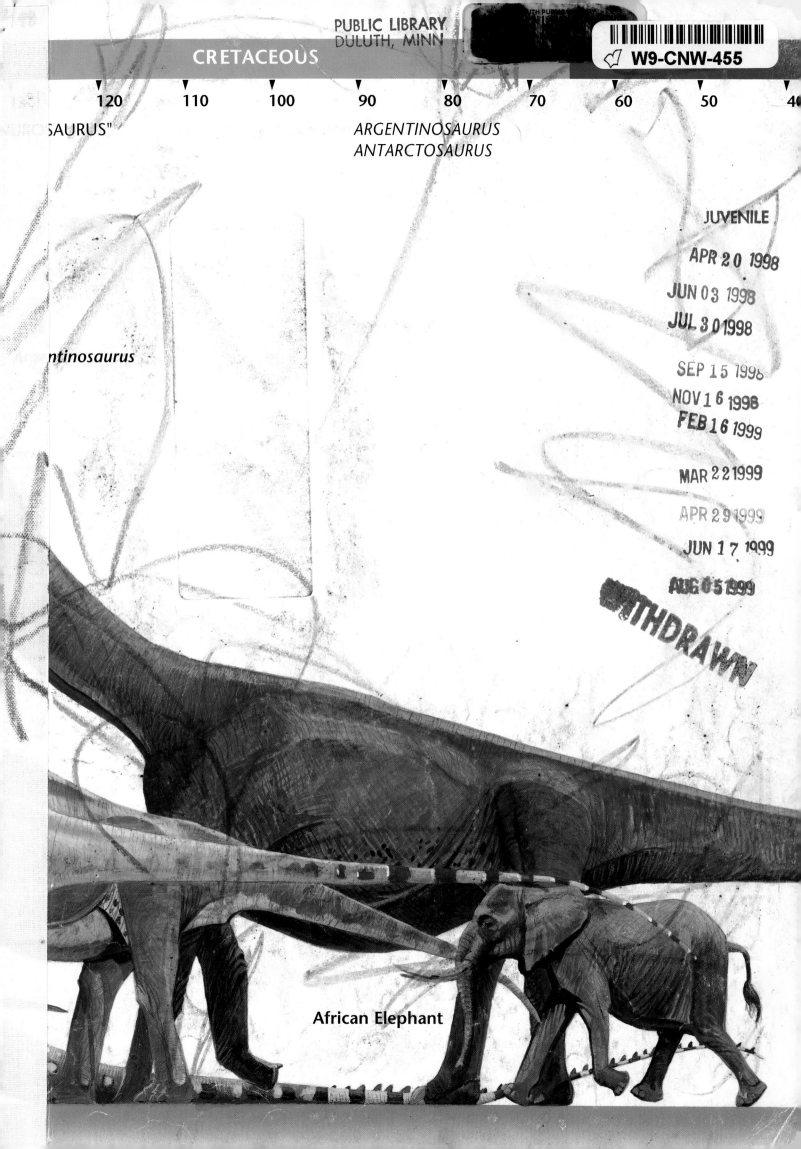

African Elephant

SUPERGIANTS!

THE BIGGEST DINOSAURS

by **Don Lessem**   Illustrated by **David Peters**

Scientific Adviser:

Professor Rodolfo Coria, Museo Carmen Funes,
Plaza Huincul, Argentina

Little, Brown and Company
Boston   New York   Toronto   London

INTRODUCTION

Step back in time 228 million years. Suddenly you are in the midst of a lush, warm world with many ferns and evergreen trees. The earth's land has not yet broken apart into the seven continents we know today; instead it stretches in one huge mass along the equator. The land is dominated by big reptiles. The largest of these—spread-legged crocodile-like creatures—are no more than twenty feet long. Other small meat-eaters include animals the size of an eight-year-old child, which stand with their legs straight beneath them, such as *Staurikosaurus* and *Eoraptor.* These are some of the first dinosaurs.

Now leap ahead eighty-three million years, to the end of the Jurassic period. North America is part of one of the earth's two super-continents. The land is warm and green but still without grass or flowers. Some meat-eating dinosaurs grow as large as the terrifying *Allosaurus,* longer than a moving van. One of these huge carnivores rumbles past you in search of prey, flashing its huge, sharp teeth.

Suddenly the ground begins to shake with the approaching footsteps of something far more gigantic. A huge shadow passes over you. You look up to see an animal the size of a six-story building looming above. The giant stands tall on four huge legs, swishing a tail as long as a school bus. With its tiny head, it reaches high into the treetops to snip off a green conifer branch.

The era of giant dinosaurs has dawned. For the next eighty million years, until dinosaurs disappear forever, enormous animals like these will shake the ground with their thundering steps. Nothing so big had ever lived on land before or has since.

Dinosaur. Say the word, and the image of a huge animal, far larger than any creature alive, leaps to mind. But the truth is, most dinosaurs were no bigger than station wagons. In fact, many were no bigger than Thanksgiving turkeys.

But even though most dinosaurs were not as big as the giants of our imagination, they were all large when compared to most living animals. Four out of five kinds of animals alive today are smaller than a chicken. Finding enough food and habitat to sustain a large body is difficult in any environment, modern or prehistoric. That any animal grew to the size of the biggest dinosaurs is amazing.

Scientists have known for many years that the biggest animal ever is a giant still living— the blue whale, which is more than one hundred feet long and can weigh as much as 150 tons. But the largest dinosaurs were the biggest *land* animals ever. By *biggest,* researchers mean not the longest but rather the one that weighed the most. So which dinosaur was the biggest?

Brachiosaurus, Seismosaurus, and *Ultra-sauros* are the dinosaurs that most books list as the largest. But a recent discovery in South America has convinced scientists that there was another plant-eating dinosaur far bigger. Paleontologists are still busy searching for and digging up its enormous bones in the remote badlands of Argentina. And although this newly discovered giant is beginning to become familiar to paleontologists, it has remained a mystery to almost everyone else . . . until now.

Turn the page, and find out about it, along with the past pretenders to the title of "biggest dinosaur."

WHAT IS A SAUROPOD?

Although many carnivorous dinosaurs grew to enormous sizes, the largest dinosaurs by far were plant-eaters. The largest theropods, or meat-eating dinosaurs, such as *Tyrannosaurus rex,* grew no longer than fifty feet. But many plant-eating dinosaurs stretched to nearly twice that length. These giants belong to a group of plant-eating dinosaurs called sauropods.

Sauropods walked on all fours on padded feet much like those of elephants, and they had long necks and tails. Their heads were tiny in comparison to their bodies—no bigger than horses' heads—and their brains were as small as golf balls. Very few had armor, slashing claws, or clubbed tails to defend themselves, as many other plant-eaters did, for their enormous size kept them safe from attack by even the largest carnivores. Sauropod teeth were small and few in number and were shaped like spoons or pencils. Since they could not have chewed well with their tiny teeth, sauropods used rocks to help them break down their food for digestion. How? They swallowed stones as large as peaches. In their gizzards, the stones tumbled about as if in a washing machine, helping to break down the plants they ate.

Scientists aren't sure why only herbivores, and not carnivores, grew so large, and only during this one period of earth's long history. Perhaps the plants were more abundant or nutritious then, and the air contained more oxygen than it does today. If so, the air and plants might have helped these dinosaurs grow to record size.

Paleontologists *do* know that, like modern plant-eaters, herbivorous dinosaurs had an easier time finding food than meat-eaters did.

They also know that these dinosaurs required especially large stomachs to break down the plant food they consumed.

Huge and slow, sauropods were often on the move, feeding on palmlike trees, ferns, and evergreens. Footprints show that these dinosaurs often traveled in herds, with their tails held off the ground. Sometimes they even swam together. Footprints also show that some sauropods sheltered their young in the center of their herds, as elephants do today.

Sauropods first appeared during the Jurassic period (208 million to 145 million years ago), the middle period of the Mesozoic era. Their ancestors were prosauropods, long-necked plant-eating dinosaurs that could move on four legs or just two. Prosauropods lived about two hundred million years ago and grew to a length of more than twenty feet. Sometime during the Early Jurassic, the first true sauropods appeared. They were creatures about twenty feet long that walked on all fours, such as *Vulcanodon.*

The first sauropod bones to be discovered were found in England in 1841. Sir Richard Owen, the British scientist who in that same year invented the word *dinosaur,* named the new creature a cetiosaur, or "whale lizard," because when the huge backbones of the animal were first uncovered, they were mistaken for the vertebrae of a whale. Dr. Owen thought they belonged to a crocodile.

In truth, the cetiosaurs were among the first plant-eating dinosaurs to show the basic sauropod features of a large body and four thick legs. Their necks were short compared

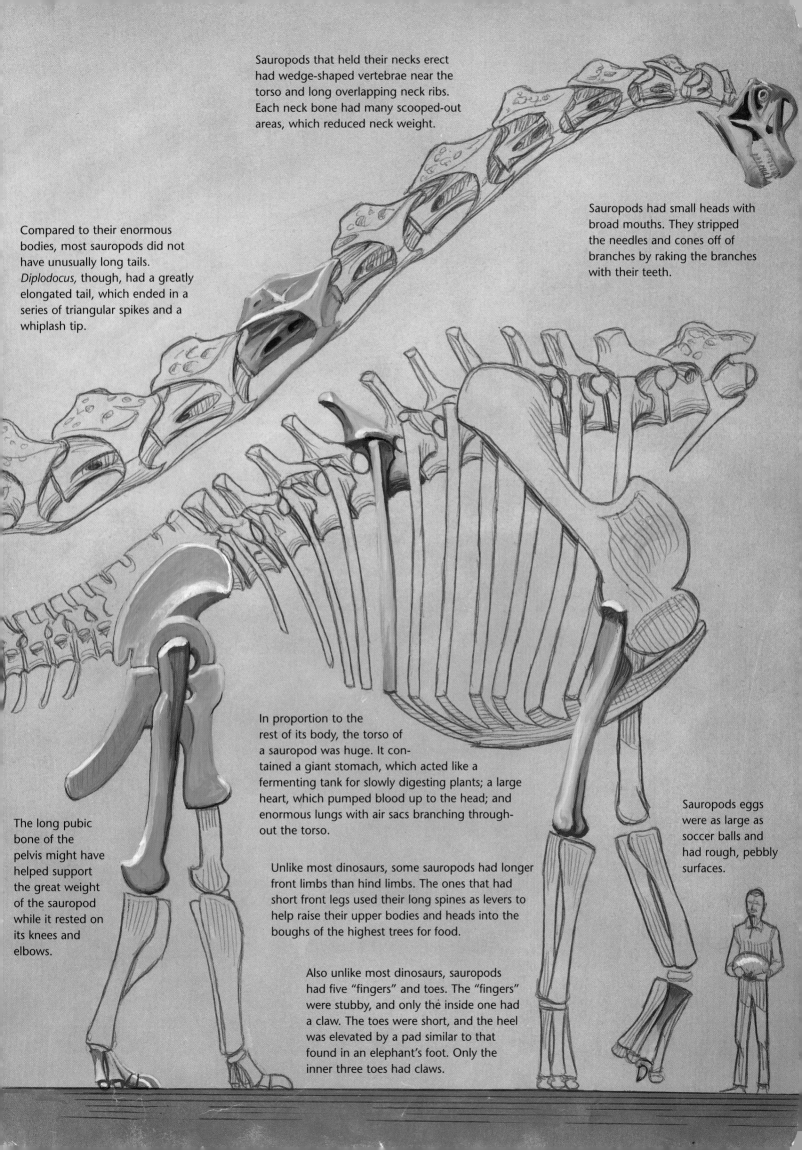

Sauropods that held their necks erect had wedge-shaped vertebrae near the torso and long overlapping neck ribs. Each neck bone had many scooped-out areas, which reduced neck weight.

Compared to their enormous bodies, most sauropods did not have unusually long tails. *Diplodocus,* though, had a greatly elongated tail, which ended in a series of triangular spikes and a whiplash tip.

Sauropods had small heads with broad mouths. They stripped the needles and cones off of branches by raking the branches with their teeth.

In proportion to the rest of its body, the torso of a sauropod was huge. It contained a giant stomach, which acted like a fermenting tank for slowly digesting plants; a large heart, which pumped blood up to the head; and enormous lungs with air sacs branching throughout the torso.

The long pubic bone of the pelvis might have helped support the great weight of the sauropod while it rested on its knees and elbows.

Sauropods eggs were as large as soccer balls and had rough, pebbly surfaces.

Unlike most dinosaurs, some sauropods had longer front limbs than hind limbs. The ones that had short front legs used their long spines as levers to help raise their upper bodies and heads into the boughs of the highest trees for food.

Also unlike most dinosaurs, sauropods had five "fingers" and toes. The "fingers" were stubby, and only the inside one had a claw. The toes were short, and the heel was elevated by a pad similar to that found in an elephant's foot. Only the inner three toes had claws.

to later sauropods, and their little heads were blunt. They lived during the early part of the Jurassic period and grew to as long as sixty feet.

The most familiar of all sauropods — *Brachiosaurus, Apatosaurus,* and *Diplodocus* — lived during the Late Jurassic period and are best known from fossils found in the American West. These dinosaurs have been known to paleontologists for more than a century. But scientists have only recently begun to sort out how these sauropods evolved and what families they belonged to. Because of the similarities in the dinosaurs' overall body shapes, scientists knew that they were closely related to each other. But many skeletons had to be uncovered, and their differences studied in detail, before scientists could begin to understand the relationships between the sauropods. Scientists are *still* sorting out what individual kinds of dinosaurs belong to which families within the sauropod group.

The biggest of the Late Jurassic sauropods are now grouped into two families: the high-necked brachiosaurids and the whip-tailed diplodocids. The brachiosaurids were built like giraffes, with front legs that were longer than their back legs and relatively short tails. They stood far taller and were more heavily built than the diplodocids, which were longer and had thin, snaking tails. Yet both families had the same basic build — big bodies set atop four large legs.

Most brachiosaurid and diplodocid fossils were discovered in the American West. But both types of dinosaurs lived in East Africa, too, since North America and East Africa were part of the same continent during the Jurassic period.

At the end of the Jurassic, the largest sauropods became extinct in North America. Duck-billed and horned dinosaurs, far smaller than the giant sauropods, became the dominant plant-eaters in North America during the last dinosaur period, the Cretaceous (145 million to 65 million years ago). These plant-

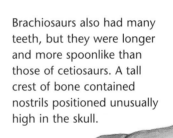

Cetiosaurs had nostrils located near the snout, an upturned jaw, and many teeth.

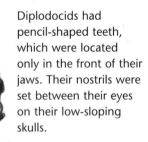

Brachiosaurs also had many teeth, but they were longer and more spoonlike than those of cetiosaurs. A tall crest of bone contained nostrils positioned unusually high in the skull.

Diplodocids had pencil-shaped teeth, which were located only in the front of their jaws. Their nostrils were set between their eyes on their low-sloping skulls.

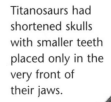

Titanosaurs had shortened skulls with smaller teeth placed only in the very front of their jaws.

eaters had teeth that were more efficient at grinding and slicing than sauropod teeth were. Perhaps that was a reason for their success in North America.

But in other parts of the world, sauropod dinosaurs continued to thrive until the end of dinosaur time. In the southern continents, especially in South America, a new family of sauropods, called titanosaurs, became the chief plant-eaters. These giants had longer back legs than front legs. They were heavily built, with relatively short tails and necks. Some had armored sides. And they were distinguished from all other sauropods by the ball-and-socket shapes of the faces of their vertebrae. Titanosaurs, whose origins were long a mystery, are now thought to have evolved from brachiosaurs.

Although their bones were among the first dinosaur fossils ever to be discovered, sauropods are still among the most mysterious of all known dinosaurs. One reason for the difficulty in sorting out these dinosaurs is that less than two dozen sauropod skulls have ever been found. Skulls provide the best clue to the evolution of an animal because they vary most in detail of any body part from one species to another. But sauropod skulls are so small and light compared to the rest of their bodies that skull bones are rarely preserved.

In addition, few complete sauropod skeletons have been found. And excavating, moving, and preparing even a few bones from such enormous creatures can take many years and cost thousands of dollars. No wonder only five scientists in the world specialize in studying sauropod dinosaurs.

But although few scientists are studying sauropods today, many sauropod fossils have been excavated for museums, which have been eager to display their enormous, crowd-pleasing skeletons. And during the past century, paleontologists and the public have made many claims as to which of these giants was the biggest dinosaur of them all. . . .

Sauropod front feet were hoof-shaped. Hind feet were broad and elephantine, with claws often pointing sideways. The distance between the left and right feet was short in most sauropods but longer in titanosaurs, which had wider hips.

THE BONE WARS

Dr. Edward Drinker Cope

The battle to find the biggest dinosaur, as well as the most dinosaurs, began in the 1870s. It was an angry contest between two American fossil scientists, Othniel Charles Marsh of Yale University and Edward Drinker Cope of Philadelphia. They began feuding in 1870, when Dr. Marsh embarrassed Dr. Cope by pointing out that he had put the head of a sea reptile, *Elasmosaurus,* on the wrong end of its skeleton!

In the late 1870s, their battle grew into what paleontologists call the "Bone Wars" when a schoolteacher, Arthur Lakes, found giant dinosaur bones near Morrison, Colorado, and sent samples to both men. In response, Dr. Marsh sent Lakes a hundred dollars and instructed him to keep his discovery a secret. Meanwhile Dr. Cope was about to write a scientific description of the bones — when Lakes told him to stop his work and instead forward the bones to Dr. Marsh.

Furious, Dr. Cope hired another schoolteacher, O. W. Lucas, to find bones for him in another promising dig site, Canyon City, Colorado. When an even better site was found by railroad workers in Wyoming, both Dr. Cope and Dr. Marsh sent crews to excavate the bones of giant dinosaurs and ship them east. At times, their workers hid bones, and even destroyed them, so rivals wouldn't find them. Some even threatened competitors with murder!

When each new fossil was uncovered, Dr. Cope and Dr. Marsh hurried to name a new dinosaur from their workers' finds, often long before they knew if the bones truly represented a new kind of animal. When the first giant sauropod was named in the Bone Wars, only a single skeleton of a giant dinosaur, *Cetiosaurus,* had been discovered. At the time, scientists had no idea that a whole group of giants, the sauropod dinosaurs, existed.

In 1877, Dr. Cope named the first giant sauropod discovered in America. It was

Camarasaurus, a plant-eater that grew to sixty feet long, as large as *Cetiosaurus.* Although the specimen lacked leg bones, Dr. Cope correctly imagined it to be a four-legged animal.

The next year, Dr. Marsh's crew found leg bones and more of the skeleton of another *Camarasaurus,* in the same area, near Canyon City, Colorado. But Dr. Marsh mistakenly thought it was a new animal and named it "Morosaurus," or "stupid lizard." Dr. Marsh thought it must have been slow-witted since the head of the dinosaur was tiny compared to its huge size. During the same year, Dr. Marsh also invented the name *sauropod,* meaning "lizard foot," to describe the giant animals. And in 1879, he named the first of the truly gigantic dinosaurs — *Diplodocus.*

Dr. Othniel Charles Marsh

DIPLODOCUS: The Whip-tailed Giant

When he created the group name *sauropod,* Dr. Marsh had in mind not just *Camarasaurus* and *Cetiosaurus* but also the first dinosaur bones found near Canyon City, Colorado, in 1877. The bones formed most of the rear end and tail of a dinosaur even larger than *Camarasaurus* and *Cetiosaurus.* This new dinosaur had some upside-down T-shaped bones hanging down from its tail vertebrae, which led Dr. Marsh to name it *Diplodocus,* or "double beam."

Two partial *Diplodocus* skeletons discovered in Wyoming in 1899, and a complete skeleton found at Dinosaur National Monument in Utah and excavated in the 1930s, gave paleontologists additional information about this giant creature. At 82½ feet long, this last skeleton is nearly as long as a basketball court. It is still the longest complete dinosaur skeleton ever found.

Diplodocus's long, slim neck and tail made up much of its length, so it did not weigh as much as other dinosaurs of similar lengths that have since been discovered. It was no lightweight, though — scientists estimate that *Diplodocus* weighed at least eleven tons, or more than two bull elephants.

Diplodocus supported its heavy weight with strong hips and legs. Five of its vertebrae were fused atop its pelvis, giving extra strength to its hips. Its legs were thick, and its front and hind feet were wide, with long toes. Wide feet and heavy legs helped to support its big body. The first specimen of *Diplodocus* was so incomplete that Dr. Marsh pictured it with the shorter-toed feet of the better-known and smaller sauropod, *Camarasaurus.* Many museums have repeated Dr. Marsh's error, mistakenly placing the feet of *Camarasaurus* on skeletons of *Diplodocus.*

In the early 1900s, scientists around the world marveled at *Diplodocus* and debated its posture. Researchers in Germany and the United States suggested that these giants must have crept along the ground. If they had stood upright, the scientists reasoned, their weight would have made them sink into the mud. And dinosaurs were still thought of as lizards, as Dr. Owen had imagined them when he gave them the name *dinosaur.* Lizards walk with their legs bent.

But the scientist who restored a skeleton of *Diplodocus,* Dr. W. J. Holland of the Carnegie Museum, in Pittsburgh, disagreed. He argued that if *Diplodocus* had walked with its legs sprawled sideways, its body would have dragged so deeply beneath it that it would have dug a trench in the ground as it walked. Dr. Holland was not proved right until the 1930s, when footprints of a sauropod dinosaur were discovered in Texas. The width of the trackway — the distance from one leg to the opposite leg across the animal's body — was only six feet. If these giants had walked with their legs sprawled, their trackway would have been much wider.

A few years after the first discovery of *Diplodocus,* Dr. Marsh's workers uncovered another giant dinosaur in the Black Hills of

South Dakota. In 1890, Dr. Marsh named this new dinosaur *Barosaurus,* meaning "heavy reptile." Although its body was the same length as *Diplodocus*'s, its neck bones were longer, making it ninety-three feet long. But with the exception of its longer neck, a slightly shorter tail, and heavier hind limbs, *Barosaurus* is nearly identical to *Diplodocus,* and many scientists think it may have been just a very large example of *Diplodocus.* The tallest mounted skeleton in the world is the fifty-foot-high rearing *Barosaurus* in the lobby of the American Museum of Natural History, in New York.

INSIDE ▶ DIPLODOCUS

FAMILY: Diplodocidae

LENGTH: 5 feet (24.8 meters)

ESTIMATED WEIGHT: 11 tons or more

PLACE: Colorado, Wyoming, Utah, Montana

PERIOD: Late Jurassic, 156 million to 145 million years ago

DIET: Evergreen tree leaves, ferns

DISTINGUISHING FEATURES:

• Long, snaking tail with 80 or more vertebrae. The 19 vertebrae closest to the hips were hollow, making the tail more maneuverable.

• Small sloped head, with teeth only in the front of the mouth. Teeth were small and peg-shaped. Nostrils were positioned above the eyes.

• Five toes on broad rear feet; large blunt claws on inside three toes.

APATOSAURUS: Don't Call It "Brontosaurus"!

In 1877, the same year that *Diplodocus* was found, its larger cousin, *Apatosaurus*, was first uncovered by Arthur Lakes in Morrison, Colorado. So began a story of giant dinosaur confusion that lasts to this day.

Dr. Marsh named the dinosaur *Apatosaurus,* or "deceptive reptile," after examining its huge hipbones and backbones. A second excavation soon produced more bones of this dinosaur. In 1879, Marsh's collectors found two similar giant skeletons in Como Bluff, Wyoming. One was an almost complete skeleton, missing only a skull. This skeleton looked much like a larger version of the one he had named *Apatosaurus.* But this new specimen had four vertebrae near its hips instead of three. Dr. Marsh did not realize, as was later discovered, that *Apatosauruses* were born with just three lower vertebrae and that a fourth one formed as the dinosaurs grew up. Dr. Marsh had found an adult *Apatosaurus,* but he thought instead that a new dinosaur had been discovered. He named it "Brontosaurus," or "thunder lizard."

In 1883, Dr. Marsh mounted the bones of "Brontosaurus," creating the first skeleton reconstruction of any giant dinosaur. However, he made many mistakes. He included the slender legs, the feet, and shorter tail and neck of a *Camarasaurus* that had been found in a quarry near the "Brontosaurus" bones at Como Bluff. And he topped off his reconstruction with the boxier skull of a *Camarasaurus* as well. Only recently have many museums corrected this error in their skeletons of this animal.

But Dr. Marsh's most confusing error of all was calling "Brontosaurus" a new animal. The mistake was recognized by paleontologist Elmer Riggs in 1903. But by then the name "Brontosaurus" had become so familiar that even today people still think it is the correct name for this large plant-eater. Since *Apatosaurus* was the first name used, though, it is the only correct scientific name for this dinosaur.

Under any name, this is an impressive animal. Its enormous tail contained eighty-two bones and was more than twenty-five feet long, the last half of it a snaking, thin whip. Its neck was shorter than *Diplodocus*'s, though, so its overall length was probably less than seventy-seven feet. But it was more heavily built than *Diplodocus,* and paleontologists estimate that it weighed nearly twice as much, perhaps twenty tons — about the same as four of the biggest elephants.

In 1910, a nearly complete skeleton of *Apatosaurus* was found near Vernal, Utah, by Earl Douglass, from Pittsburgh's Carnegie Museum. Mr. Douglass later found parts of many other dinosaurs at the site now known as Dinosaur National Monument. Among the fossil remains were the bones of three young apatosaurs. Later discoveries showed that many sauropods sheltered their young in the center of their herds, protecting them from predators, which is probably why these three youngsters were grouped together. But the fossils that washed into the bottom of the ancient stream channel that is now the rock of Dinosaur National Monument offer no evidence of what *Apatosaurus* family life was like.

Without evidence, the first scientists to study *Apatosaurus* imagined a far different creature than the one we know today. When Dr. Marsh made his first drawings of a

INSIDE ▶ APATOSAURUS
Also known as "Brontosaurus"

FAMILY: Diplodocidae

LENGTH: 73.2 to 76.6 feet (22 to 23 meters)

ESTIMATED WEIGHT: 17 to 20 tons

PLACE: Colorado, Utah, Oklahoma, Wyoming, Baja California, Mexico

PERIOD: Late Jurassic, 156 million to 145 million years ago

DIET: Tree leaves, ferns

DISTINGUISHING FEATURES:

• A low, sloping head like that of *Diplodocus,* with similar pencil-shaped teeth

• Neck vertebrae thicker and heavier than those of *Diplodocus*

sauropod, he used the animal he called "Brontosaurus" as his model. He concluded that it was "stupid, slow-moving," and "more or less amphibious." These statements by the leading dinosaur scientist of the time created a lasting popular view of dinosaurs as swamp-dwelling pea-brained giants.

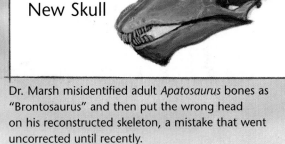

Old Skull

New Skull

Dr. Marsh misidentified adult *Apatosaurus* bones as "Brontosaurus" and then put the wrong head on his reconstructed skeleton, a mistake that went uncorrected until recently.

AMPHICOELIAS: THE GIANT THAT GOT AWAY

The longest dinosaur ever is one that was found, then lost. In 1877, Dr. Cope had named the first species of the giant sauropod *Amphicoelias* from a backbone, thighbone, and part of a hip discovered in Canyon City, home to so many sauropod fossils. This dinosaur, *Amphicoelias altus* (the name means "both hollow and tall"), was estimated to have grown to about 86$\frac{1}{2}$ feet in length and to have weighed twelve tons. It was slightly larger and heavier than *Diplodocus* but similar in its long tail and relatively slim build.

The next year, Dr. Cope's workers discovered a similar backbone fossil in Morrison, Colorado. Dr. Cope believed that this new bone belonged to a dinosaur that was also an *Amphicoelias.* But because it was far larger than the backbone found the year before, Dr. Cope thought that it was from a different species. So he declared a new dinosaur, naming it *Amphicoelias fragillimus* ("both hollow and fragile"). The fragile arch on the top of the backbone was taller than a man! Judging from the measurements Dr. Cope made of this single bone, modern scientists estimate that *Amphicoelias fragillimus* was the longest dinosaur by far of any yet known. It was at least 125 feet long and perhaps as long as 200 feet—longer than two basketball courts!

From examining drawings, experts now consider this gigantic bone to be the typically hollowed backbone of a *Diplodocus*-type dinosaur. But it probably was not a different species of *Amphicoelias* and perhaps was just a very large *Diplodocus*. Paleontologists can't be certain, for no additional fossils from this dinosaur have ever been found, and the fossil that Dr. Cope reported has disappeared.

What happened to the giant bone? No one knows. Dr. Cope kept many of his fossils in the basement of his house, and the delicate bone

of *Amphicoelias fragillimus* may have simply crumbled. Or it may have been misplaced.

Although its backbone fossil has long been lost, *Amphicoelias fragillimus* is still important to the history of dinosaur science, for it was the first giant sauropod to be depicted as it

Charles R. Knight portrayed *Amphicoelias* as an aquatic dinosaur.

might have looked while alive. In 1897, with Dr. Cope's guidance, Charles R. Knight, the great dinosaur artist of the American Museum of Natural History, painted a group of *Amphicoelias* dinosaurs. He pictured them with bodies underwater and heads sticking up above the surface, allowing them to breathe as they fed on plants in the swampy rivers.

Knight's view of sauropod dinosaurs as swamp-bound giants came from Drs. Cope and Marsh and from other scientists of his time, who thought these animals were so huge that they could not possibly have supported their own weight walking on land. The only way these creatures could have moved, scientists thought, was by walking in water, which would have helped support some of their enormous weight. Scientists pointed to the placement of the nostrils on many sauropods—on top of, rather than at the front of, their skulls—evidence for their theory. With nostrils atop their heads, sauropods could breathe even while partially submerged.

Detailed studies done in the 1970s of plant fossils and the rocks in which *Amphicoelias* and other giant dinosaurs were buried showed that Dr. Marsh and his fellow scientists were wrong. Much of the American West at the end of the Jurassic period was dry and not at all swampy. Sauropods walked through forests, eating plants, and they died in or near streams, not swamps. But Mr. Knight's painting was so influential that artists, filmmakers, and the public have believed until only quite recently that the giant dinosaurs lived only in swampy waters.

Amphicoelias fragillimus

FAMILY: Diplodocidae

LENGTH: 125 to 200 feet (40 to 65 meters)

ESTIMATED WEIGHT: 50 to 150 tons

PLACE: Colorado

PERIOD: Late Jurassic, 156 million to 145 million years ago

DIET: Evergreen plants and palmlike plants called cycads

DISTINGUISHING FEATURE: A complete vertebra probably would have measured between 10 and 13 feet high. Its vertebrae were also unusually narrow.

If such a dinosaur as *Amphicoelias fragillimus* did exist, it would have dwarfed humans, animals, and most dinosaurs.

BRACHIOSAURUS: THE GIANT GIRAFFE?

Brachiosaurus was discovered almost a century ago. But to this day, no larger nearly complete dinosaur skeleton has ever been found. The first bones of *Brachiosaurus* ("arm reptile") were just isolated pieces, discovered in 1900 in the Grand River valley of western Colorado. They were named by Chicago scientist Elmer Riggs. Much more complete remains of *Brachiosaurus* were uncovered in 1907 in what is now Tanzania, in East Africa. The Berlin Museum of Natural History mounted an expedition to the site from 1908 to 1912 and collected more than 250 tons of *Brachiosaurus* fossils. A skeleton was built from them, which measured thirty-nine feet tall and seventy-four feet in length—the most massive dinosaur skeleton ever displayed.

Brachiosaurus was among the heaviest of all dinosaurs, even though its backbones had large holes in their sides to reduce their weight, as did the vertebrae of other giant sauropods. But *Brachiosaurus* had several features peculiar to it among giant dinosaurs. It had a relatively short tail and a very wide, thick body. Its front feet were long and narrow, and its skull featured huge nostrils, which may have been used for cooling its head, producing loud noises, or giving the animal a keen sense of smell.

But the most unusual feature of *Brachiosaurus* was the length of its leg bones. As the first *Brachiosaurus* was being excavated, Dr. Riggs initially mistook the upper arm bones of this dinosaur for its thighbones. It was an understandable mistake, for unlike all other known sauropods, this dinosaur had longer front limbs than back. Its upper arm bone, which measured eighty inches, was actually an inch longer than its thighbone. Dr. Riggs discovered his error as more of the bones were uncovered. The wide end of the longer bones showed clearly that these were upper arm bones.

Here was a sauropod dinosaur with a very different body than those previously found. Like a giraffe, its front legs were longer than its hind limbs, supporting a high chest. The body of this dinosaur was also much sturdier, suggesting that this animal weighed much more than any dinosaur yet known.

But unlike modern amphibious creatures, such as hippopotamuses, these dinosaurs had narrow, deep chests and hollowed-out backbones. Dr. Riggs argued that the giant dinosaurs must have lived on land, perhaps rearing up on their hind legs to feed high in trees. Although most dinosaur scientists of his time disagreed with Dr. Riggs, modern paleontologists concur with Dr. Riggs's conclusions about the lifestyle of sauropods.

Did *Brachiosaurus* hold its neck up high to feed in trees? It is now commonly pictured that way. But *Brachiosaurus* had no forked spines on its neck vertebrae, as other sauropods had. Paleontologists think that these spines were attachment points for large neck ligaments, which might have helped sauropods hold their necks up high. The absence of these ligaments on *Brachiosaurus* leads some scientists to speculate that this dinosaur did not have the strength to hold its head high in the treetops.

There is yet another problem with *Brachiosaurus* keeping its head up high—pumping blood to its head. Creating enough blood pressure to bring blood to the brain when the animal's head was raised four stories in the air would require a circulatory system unlike that known in any living animal. Giraffes rely on a series of valves in their necks to help push blood to their heads. Perhaps *Brachiosaurus* had a similar system. It's just one of the many mysteries we may never solve about how these dinosaurs were built and how they behaved.

INSIDE ▷ Brachiosaurus

FAMILY: Brachiosauridae

LENGTH: 66.6 to 83.2 feet long (20 to 25 meters)

ESTIMATED WEIGHT: 30 to 50 tons

PLACE: Colorado, Wyoming, Utah, Tanzania, possibly Algeria and Portugal

PERIOD: Late Jurassic, 156 million to 145 million years ago

DIET: Branches and needles of conifers (including those at treetop level), cycads, ferns

DISTINGUISHING FEATURES:

• Blunt skull; chisel-shaped teeth with marks of wear, indicating that it chewed tough plants

• A tiny brain, which weighed one hundred thousand times less than the dinosaur's body

• A relatively short tail for a giant sauropod

• Front legs that were narrow and long— longer than its back limbs

ANTARCTOSAURUS: THE SOUTHERN GIANT

At the turn of the twentieth century, the scene of new giant dinosaur discoveries shifted to South America. Huge dinosaur bones had been discovered in Argentina as early as the late 1800s, and in 1916 an Argentinean fossil prospector named Wichmann uncovered several bones from what would prove to be a dinosaur far larger than any discovered previously. But it was not until the German paleontologist Friedrich von Huene visited South America to study these and other fossils that scientists realized just how enormous an animal Dr. Wichmann had uncovered.

After examining the bones of this giant dinosaur, which included a shoulder blade, leg bones, two vertebrae, parts of the hips, and a small piece of jaw with several teeth, Dr. von Huene named the new dinosaur *Antarctosaurus wichmannianus*. Dr. von Huene also named an even larger species of *Antarctosaurus*, which he called *giganteus*, based on a huge pair of thighbones and shinbones found in another quarry. The thighbones of this animal were slender but measured more than six feet in length. Scientists today feel that too little of this giant dinosaur is known to determine if it is really a separate species of *Antarctosaurus*.

Antarctosaurus was a member of a still-mysterious group of giant sauropod dinosaurs called titanosaurs. These sauropods are distinguished by the ball-and-socket shape of their tail vertebrae, which differs from the flatter vertebrae sides of other giant sauropods. Also, unlike its fellow sauropods, no complete skeleton or skull of a titanosaur has ever been found. These incomplete fossils make studying this family of giant dinosaurs very difficult. From the titanosaur fossils that have been found, though, paleontologists can see that these dinosaurs had short tails. Their hind legs were also as long or longer than their front legs. Titanosaurs have long been grouped with the diplodocid dinosaurs, but many modern scientists now question whether these two groups are closely related.

Some titanosaurs were less than thirty feet long, which is small for sauropods. But others were enormous. They appeared in Asia, Africa, Europe, and, for a brief period at the end of dinosaur time, in North America but were most common in South America.

Dr. von Huene was one of the few experts on titanosaurs. By studying them, and the fossils of other animals and plants that lived in South America during the last period of dinosaur time, he was able to devise new theories about the environment during this period. His studies revealed that in low tropical land near the sea, giant sauropods lived to the very end of dinosaur time, sixty-five million years ago, far later than had previously been thought.

Despite Dr. von Huene's pioneering studies, little is known about the lifestyle of *Antarctosaurus* or other titanosaurs. At the time of his studies, *Antarctosaurus* was the biggest dinosaur ever discovered. And for more than fifty years, there was no reason to think that any bigger dinosaur would ever be found. . . .

INSIDE ▶ ## Antarctosaurus

FAMILY: Titanosauridae

LENGTH: Up to 100 feet (35 meters)

ESTIMATED WEIGHT: 50 tons

PLACE: Chile, Uruguay, Argentina

PERIOD: Late Cretaceous, 83 million to 65 million years ago

DIET: Evergreen trees, ferns

DISTINGUISHING FEATURES:

• Tiny head, just two feet long and very high, with big eyeholes and weak jaws

• Primitive thin teeth, slab-shaped, without sharp edges

• Ball-and-socket-shaped tail vertebrae; probably helped to support its tail

• Sturdily built legs with hind legs longer than front legs

MAMENCHISAURUS AND "NUROSAURUS":
THE CHINESE GIANTS

Due to a shortage of scientists and funds, dinosaur explorations in western countries declined in the middle of the twentieth century. But in China, a country rich in dinosaurs from many periods, a new era of dinosaur exploration has flourished since the end of World War II, in 1945.

Dr. Yang Chung Chien was China's leading fossil scientist after the war. He discovered many new kinds of dinosaurs across China from all three periods of dinosaur time. But in the early 1950s, his largest discovery was presented to him. Construction workers had found huge dinosaur bones while building a bridge across a brook called Mamenchi in central China. Work was stopped, and Dr. Yang was called in. His crew excavated what proved to be a giant sauropod dinosaur with an amazingly long neck. Although the entire spine of the animal was unearthed, along with many of its limb bones, its skull and feet were not found.

Still, Dr. Yang had plenty of evidence to declare this a new kind of dinosaur, which he did in 1954, calling it *Mamenchisaurus,* or "lizard from Mamenchi." *Mamenchisaurus* lived more than 160 million years ago, earlier than *Diplodocus.* But in many ways, the two were similar, especially in the shape of their tail and neck vertebrae and in their overall length.

But *Mamenchisaurus* was distinguished by its remarkable neck. While many sauropod dinosaurs had twelve neck vertebrae, *Mamenchisaurus* had nineteen. They supported a neck that was at least thirty-three feet long. That's more than a third of the total length of the animal's body and longer than the neck of any other animal, ever!

How *Mamenchisaurus* held and used that neck is unknown. Some scientists and artists picture it reaching high into trees to feed. But most think it unlikely that this dinosaur could have held its enormous neck high for long. Instead, it may have used it to find plants by sweeping it far across the landscape, like the hose of a vacuum cleaner.

More than thirty years after *Mamenchisaurus* was discovered, Dr. Yang's former student

Dr. Dong Zhiming found an even bigger specimen of the dinosaur. On a joint expedition with Canadian scientists in the far northwest of China, Dr. Dong excavated part of the neck of what appeared to be a *Mamenchisaurus*. He estimates that this dinosaur was one hundred feet in length, the longest dinosaur ever found in Asia. The neck alone may have been more than forty feet long!

In 1991, Dr. Dong and workers in Chinese Inner Mongolia excavated most of a huge sauropod dinosaur from far later in dinosaur time. This creature lived in the Early Cretaceous, the last dinosaur period, about thirty million years or more after *Mamenchisaurus*. It has not yet been scientifically described and for now has been grouped with *Mamenchisaurus*, though Dr. Dong thinks it may have been more closely related to *Camarasaurus*. But its limb proportions are most like *Brachiosaurus*. Since much of China appears to have been isolated during most of dinosaur time, it makes sense to scientists that its sauropods would evolve in a way that was peculiar to that region.

This giant dinosaur has acquired an unofficial name, "Nurosaurus." Since "Nurosaurus" was more solidly built than *Mamenchisaurus* or *Diplodocus*, this eighty-five-foot-long skeleton is perhaps the largest ever reconstructed. But it has yet to be scientifically studied. Chinese scientists are in such dire need of money that they had to send the fossil off for exhibit in wealthier countries such as the United States in order to raise funds to study it.

INSIDE ▶ **Mamenchisaurus**

LENGTH: 82 feet (25 meters), possibly up to 100 feet (35 meters)

ESTIMATED WEIGHT: 14 to 26.6 tons

PLACE: China

PERIOD: Middle Jurassic, 160 million years ago

DIET: Evergreen trees, cycads, ferns

DISTINGUISHING FEATURES:

• Skull higher and blunter than that of *Diplodocus*

• Teeth were more spoon-shaped and stronger than *Diplodocus*'s

• Tail had upside-down T-shaped chevrons, like those of *Diplodocus*

SUPERSAURUS AND ULTRASAUROS:
BIGGER DINOSAURS OUT WEST?

"Dinosaur Jim" Jensen is one of the great dinosaur hunters. Mr. Jensen began dreaming about digging giant dinosaurs when he was ten. After high school, he worked as a mechanic at the scientific laboratories of Harvard University. He took a great interest in fossils and joined Harvard scientists on expeditions from Argentina to Antarctica. Then, in middle age, he moved back to his native Utah to dig dinosaurs for Brigham Young University.

From the 1960s to the 1980s, Dinosaur Jim dug enough bones to fill most of the huge room underneath the bleachers of the university's football stadium. Many of them came from a quarry called Dry Mesa, in the mountains of western Colorado, where fossils are still being discovered after thirty summers of digging. In 1971, Mr. Jensen began digging in the quarry, looking for the biggest of all meat-eating dinosaurs. Instead he found the biggest plant-eaters.

At this first Dry Mesa dig, Jensen's grown son Ron discovered the shoulder blade of an enormous dinosaur, one far larger than any other such dinosaur bone yet discovered. The shape of this bone led Jim Jensen to conclude that this new dinosaur bone was related to *Diplodocus*. Based on the evidence of the shoulder blade, he estimated that this new animal measured between 117 feet and 150 feet from head to tail and was over fifty-four feet tall. Other paleontologists think Mr. Jensen's estimates are too high. But they still conclude that this was an enormous dinosaur, the largest member of the diplodocid family ever discovered.

Only a few other parts of the animal Jensen called *Supersaurus* have since been found: some neck ribs and a pelvis. The pelvis is six feet long and six feet wide and weighs 1,500 pounds. It is the largest single chunk of dinosaur bone ever found.

But we already know there were bigger dinosaurs than *Supersaurus* at Dry Mesa. In 1979, Jim Jensen was digging again at the quarry when his crew found another enormous shoulder blade from a sauropod dinosaur. This bone was nearly nine feet long and much broader than the shoulder blade of *Supersaurus*. Jensen was immediately convinced that he had discovered the largest dinosaur of all, because this shoulder blade was similar in shape but larger than that of the heaviest dinosaur then known, *Brachiosaurus*. This animal would not have been as long as the whip-tailed diplodocid *Supersaurus*. But its similarities to *Brachiosaurus* indicated that it was far heavier than *Supersaurus* or any other member of the diplodocid family.

Jensen named the creature *Ultrasaurus* ("beyond lizard" and now called *Ultrasauros* because the earlier name had been previously claimed for another animal). Again, not much more of this dinosaur was found in Dry Mesa, only a backbone and possible neck vertebra. Other scientists aren't convinced that *Ultrasauros* was not just a very large *Brachiosaurus*. But even if it is just a new example of a known dinosaur, it was the largest dinosaur yet known — a creature longer than a tennis court and heavier than ten bull elephants. If it lived today, it would be able to look into a six-story window.

To scientists, what is most interesting about the huge chunks of *Ultrasauros* and *Supersaurus* and several other large dinosaurs found at Dry Mesa is what they indicate about the dinosaur community at this time and place. In the forests of the American West 145 million years ago, several kinds of sauropod dinosaurs lived at the same time. Perhaps they even lived and ate side by side, the brachiosaurs reaching high in the trees, the diplodocids feeding lower down.

INSIDE ▶ SUPERSAURUS

FAMILY: Diplodocidae

LENGTH: 117 to 150 feet long (35 to 45 meters)

ESTIMATED WEIGHT: 40 to 50 tons

PLACE: Colorado

PERIOD: Late Jurassic, 156 million to 145 million years ago

DIET: Evergreen plants, cycads, ferns

DISTINGUISHING FEATURES:

• Shoulder blade similar in shape to *Diplodocus*'s but wider at bottom

• Tail vertebrae most similar to *Barosaurus* but lacking grooves

INSIDE ▶ ULTRASAUROS

FAMILY: Brachiosauridae

LENGTH: 80 to 90 feet long

ESTIMATED WEIGHT: 40 to 50 tons

PLACE: Colorado

PERIOD: Late Jurassic, 156 million to 145 million years ago

DIET: Evergreen plants (including those at treetop level), cycads, ferns

DISTINGUISHING FEATURES:

• Its shoulder blade is the same general broad shape as that of *Brachiosaurus*.

• Its backbone is similar in the shape of its arches and spines to that of *Brachiosaurus*.

SEISMOSAURUS: THE LONGEST DINOSAUR?

Mr. Jensen's record for the longest, and perhaps the heaviest, dinosaur did not last long. A new contender for the title of longest dinosaur appeared in the late 1970s, when a group of backpackers in northern New Mexico came upon some enormous dinosaur fossils in the crumbling side of a hill.

The hikers reported their find to Dr. David Gillette, then a paleontologist at the New Mexico Museum of Natural History and now Utah's state supervisor of paleontology. In 1985, Dr. Gillette and his crew began digging into the hard sandstone where the bones were found. Unlike Dry Mesa, this site was not a jumble of

echoes for signs that the waves had struck bone. Magnetometers measured the magnetic field of the ground for disturbances produced by fossils. Even ultraviolet light generators were used to help locate fossils, which glow under this kind of light.

None of these high-tech methods worked nearly as well as old-fashioned digging with shovels and picks. But over several summers, Dr. Gillette and his team were able to remove most of the rear half of the dinosaur, except for its hind legs. They also found many polished stones near what had been the dinosaur's stomach area. These were gastroliths, rocks swallowed by the dinosaur to help grind food in its huge stomach. One

bones. Instead, Dr. Gillette soon discovered, much of an enormous dinosaur skeleton was buried in the rock.

To remove this dinosaur was backbreaking work that took Dr. Gillette and large crews of assistants several summers to complete. Dynamite was used to remove many tons of rock over the fossils.

In an ambitious experiment in new dinosaur-hunting techniques, high-tech devices were tried to locate the fossils. Gamma ray detectors measured radioactivity, since many fossils concentrate the radioactive element uranium within them. Shotguns blasted sound waves into the ground, and scientists listened with hydrophones to the

particularly large stone was the size of a tennis ball. Dr. Gillette speculated jokingly that this dinosaur choked to death after swallowing this too-large rock.

After many months of excavating the bones, Dr. Gillette began to realize how enormous this dinosaur was. He made detailed measurements of the bones his crew found and compared them with those of *Ultrasauros* and *Supersaurus*. Only then did he realize that judging from its tailbones, this animal was at least one quarter longer than any dinosaur known.

He gave this new dinosaur a name fit for a giant: *Seismosaurus,* or "earth shaker lizard." The size of the tail vertebrae indicated to

Dr. Gillette that this dinosaur was at least 110 feet long and perhaps as long as 170 feet. Although some other scientists don't think this *Seismosaurus* individual was any longer than 125 feet, it is still the longest dinosaur known.

What kind of sauropod was *Seismosaurus?* Dr. Gillette and other scientists think *Seismosaurus* was closely related to the whip-tailed diplodocids, judging from the shape of its long tail and the T-shaped bones that dangle from both animals' tail vertebrae.

Seismosaurus was the longest of dinosaurs, but it was not the biggest. The stocky brachiosaurs, including *Ultrasauros,* were perhaps twice its weight.

And before *Seismosaurus* was officially named in 1992, scientists in South America were busy digging another dinosaur nearly as long as *Seismosaurus* and heavier than *Ultrasauros.* But they didn't know then how enormous that dinosaur would prove to be. . . .

INSIDE ▶ Seismosaurus

FAMILY: Diplodocidae

LENGTH: 110 to 170 feet

ESTIMATED WEIGHT: 25 to 30 tons

PLACE: New Mexico

PERIOD: Late Jurassic, 156 million to 145 million years ago

DIET: Evergreens, cycads, and ferns

DISTINGUISHING FEATURES:

• Tail vertebrae most like those of *Diplodocus,* though more paddle-shaped

• Legs thought to be short because of stubby pubic bone

Gastroliths, or stomach stones, taken from the *Seismosaurus* quarry. The stones, polished from weeks, months, or years in *Seismosaurus*'s gizzard, ranged in size from 1 to 4.25 inches in width.

ARGENTINOSAURUS: THE NEW CHAMPION

In 1987, a rancher was walking along the road to the nearby city of Plaza Huincul in the center of Argentina. Amid the scrubby bushes and large pebbles on the dry ground, the rancher saw a dark object shaped like a log. He tried to lift it, but it was as heavy as stone. The rancher thought it must be petrified wood. He'd found many smaller pieces of such wood nearby.

The rancher was puzzled enough by the slab to contact a scientist at the museum in Plaza Huincul, who came to examine it. The scientist thought it wasn't petrified wood but a fossil — the bone of a dinosaur. Professor Jose Bonaparte, Argentina's leading fossil scientist, was called in from Buenos Aires, several hundred miles away, to examine the rancher's find.

Prof. Bonaparte came to the site and immediately realized that the log-shaped slab was the nearly six-foot-high fossilized leg bone of a giant sauropod. Because of its great size, he assumed it was the dinosaur's thigh-bone. This bone would have belonged to a big dinosaur, but not the biggest ever, for several other sauropods had larger thigh-bones.

Still, Prof. Bonaparte and his assistant Rodolfo Coria were eager to investigate the site further. The next year, Bonaparte returned to begin the search for more of the dinosaur's bones. Before long, he came upon several of its backbones. Each backbone was enormous — five feet high and just as wide. With picks and pneumatic drills, he and his assistants excavated the bones from the hard, pebbly sandstone. Each backbone weighed a ton, making the job of moving them enormously difficult. After Prof. Bonaparte coated the bones and surrounding rock with a cast of plaster soaked in bandages, workers on trucks hauled the bones out with winches.

Another large fossil of the animal that Prof. Bonaparte uncovered was the sacrum, a bone at the top of the pelvis. This bone was narrower in the front than in the back, a feature not seen in most other sauropod dinosaurs.

Bonaparte also found some of the enormous ribs of the dinosaur. While other dinosaurs' ribs are flat in shape, like human ribs, these ribs were as rounded as mailing tubes.

And while most plant-eating dinosaurs had spongy bones, the bones of this dinosaur appeared to be hollowed out in many places.

Prof. Bonaparte knew he was digging up an enormous dinosaur. But how big a dinosaur, and what kind of sauropod it was, he could not decide until he had cleaned and prepared the bones he had found. And he knew he would need to explore the site further, for the tips of dinosaur bones could be seen protruding from the dusty ground for many yards in all directions.

Professor Rodolfo Coria

A chunk of fossilized *Argentinosaurus* bone found at the dig site

FIGURING OUT THE GIANT

In 1989, Professor Rodolfo Coria moved to Plaza Huincul and became the city's official paleontologist, so that he could further study and dig up this mysterious giant dinosaur. Over many summers he excavated more of the dinosaur and hauled the plastered bones back to the Museo Carmen Funes, the city museum.

By 1995, Prof. Coria had uncovered and cleaned several backbones, ribs, and parts of the dinosaur's hips and rear leg. Prof. Bonaparte and he had written the first scientific description of the dinosaur in 1993 and given it an official name: *Argentinosaurus.*

Prof. Bonaparte had grouped this dinosaur outside the titanosaurs, even though they were the only other giant dinosaurs known from Argentina. But after studying more of the bones and visiting scientists and fossil collections in North America, Prof. Coria came to a more specific conclusion.

The sacrum, or upper pelvic bone, of *Argentinosaurus* was shaped like that of a brachiosaur, not a titanosaur. The backbones also looked more like those of a brachiosaur than those of a titanosaur.

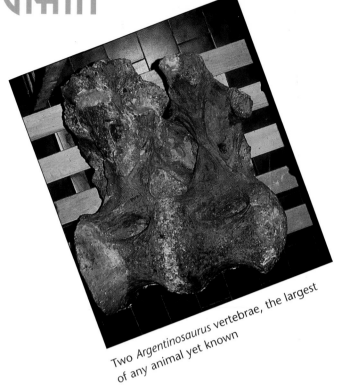

Two *Argentinosaurus* vertebrae, the largest of any animal yet known

And the leg bone of *Argentinosaurus* had a bootlike shape at its bottom. That shape was unlike any leg bone of a titanosaur but was similar to a brachiosaur shinbone.

So Prof. Coria concluded that this dinosaur belonged between brachiosaurs and titanosaurs in evolution. This decision was very important to other scientists, since it suggested how titanosaurs might have originated. The giant brachiosaurs of North America lived long before the titanosaurs best known from South America. *Argentinosaurus* lived midway in time between the brachiosaurs and the titanosaurs. Maybe it was a link between the two in the evolution of titanosaurs.

Prof. Coria's discovery meant something more. Since the leg bone was a shin, a smaller bone than the thigh on any sauropod, then *Argentinosaurus* was far larger than first thought. The enormous backbones he had uncovered also indicated that this animal was a possible record setter. They were larger than any complete backbones ever found.

Prof. Coria compared the size of these bones to those of *Brachiosaurus* and titanosaurs. *Argentinosaurus,* he estimated, was 110 feet long, longer than any well-preserved dinosaur except *Seismosaurus. Argentinosaurus* might have weighed as much as one hundred tons.

Prof. Coria discovered that to support its incredible size and weight, *Argentinosaurus*

Drilling into sandstone to excavate a huge *Argentinosaurus* vertebra half-buried in rock

had developed several unusual features. Its ribs were cylindrical, giving this gigantic dinosaur strength without burdening it with overwhelming weight. Its vertebrae contained many holes and spongy parts to lighten their weight. And an extra set of struts to the ones found on other sauropod vertebrae helped link *Argentinosaurus*'s backbones and support its heavy midsection.

From his study of the site where *Argentinosaurus* was found, Prof. Coria was able to make some conclusions about the environment in which this dinosaur lived and died. Only a fast-moving river could have moved such heavy bones and created a sandy bottom full of large stones. The petrified wood around the site showed that the stream had flowed through a forest of tall evergreen trees called arucarians. Sometimes known as monkey-puzzle trees, they are peculiar-looking trees with swirls of high branches. *Argentinosaurus* would have had to reach high into these trees with its long neck in order to find branches to nibble.

The bones found by Prof. Coria offer only clues, not answers, to the appearance of this dinosaur. Brachiosaurs' front legs are longer than their back legs. Titanosaurs' back legs are longer than their front legs. *Argentinosaurus,* which is in between the two in size and some features, may have had four legs of equal length.

But there is more to be learned about *Argentinosaurus,* and answers are coming fast. In the spring of 1995, an American company, Knowledge Adventure, which makes educational computer games for children, donated money to support Prof. Coria's excavations. In the summer of 1995, he returned to the excavation site with more workers and gas-powered drills. Five assistants dug away at the pebbly sandstone of the ancient riverbed in which the giant's bones had been scattered. After only a few days, they had excavated two tons of fossil-rich rock.

Rebecca Lessem, age thirteen and five feet tall, stands next to the shinbone and model thighbone of *Argentinosaurus* in the Museo Carmen Funes, in Plaza Huincul, Argentina.

During the following days, fossil preparators in the museum picked away at the block with small chisels and found part of the pubic bone—one of the important hipbones—of *Argentinosaurus.*

In the second month, a three-ton block was dug out with the hope of finding another vertebra inside. The rock produced only a few fragments of bone, but one of those fragments appears to be a piece of the dinosaur's skull, a rare and valuable find, which will help Prof. Coria learn more about its appearance and evolution.

So the search goes on, month by month, day after day in the harsh, windy desert. Perhaps one day Prof. Coria will find nearly all of *Argentinosaurus.* But this particular skeleton may be so scattered that no one can ever find it all. Prof. Coria is pledged to go on looking, no matter how long and how big the job—or the dinosaur.

INSIDE ▶ Argentinosaurus

FAMILY: Titanosauridae

LENGTH: 100 to 115 feet (35 to 40 meters)

ESTIMATED WEIGHT: 80 to 100 tons

PLACE: Argentina

PERIOD: Late Cretaceous, 90 million years ago

DIET: Arucarian conifer trees

DISTINGUISHING FEATURES:

• Wing-shaped vertebrae, five feet wide and high, with a spongy interior like that of titanosaurs; additional struts for support

• Sacrum narrowing from front to back as in brachiosaurs

• Bootlike lump at base of shin, typical of brachiosaurs

AFTERWORD
Big, Bigger, Biggest?

So what is the biggest dinosaur that ever lived? *Argentinosaurus* may prove to be. But the history of discovering giant dinosaurs has taught us that new contenders for the title of biggest dinosaur keep appearing. That's not surprising, since half of all the dinosaurs we know have been discovered in the last twenty years. The pace of discovery is accelerating. In recent years, a new kind of dinosaur has been found, on average, every seven weeks.

Dinosaurs walked the earth for 165 million years. Giant plant-eating dinosaurs shook the ground for at least 120 million of those years. But scientists have been looking for dinosaurs for less than two hundred years. Only about 360 kinds of dinosaurs have been discovered to date. It is very likely that a dinosaur even bigger than *Argentinosaurus* is still in the ground, waiting to be discovered. Maybe you can be the one to find it.

How big will it be? We don't know the upper limits of animal size. With their strong muscles and hollowed bones, dinosaurs could well have grown far larger than any animal we know today.

Whatever made the giant dinosaurs grow so large, their kind will never come again. Once an animal is extinct, it can never return to life. Dinosaurs have been extinct for sixty-five million years. Perhaps one day some other kind of animal even larger than dinosaurs will evolve. But for now, we can only wonder at — and look for more fossils of — the biggest animals that ever walked the earth.

RESOURCES

BOOKS

Lambert, David. *The Ultimate Dinosaur Book.* New York: Dorling Kindersley, 1993.

Lessem, Don, and Donald F. Glut. *The Dinosaur Society Dinosaur Encyclopedia.* New York: Random House, 1994.

Norman, Dr. David. *The Illustrated Dinosaur Encyclopedia.* Illustrated by John Sibbick. New York: Crescent, 1985.

CD-ROMS

Microsoft Dinosaurs. Redmond, Washington: Microsoft, 1992.

3-D Dinosaur Adventure. Knowledge Adventure. Glendale, California: Knowledge Adventure, 1995.

Prehistoria. New York: Grolier, 1993.

Where to See Giant Dinosaur Fossils, Skeletons, and Skeleton Casts

UNITED STATES

American Museum of Natural History, New York: *Apatosaurus, Barosaurus*

Brigham Young University Museum, Provo, Utah: *Supersaurus, Ultrasauros*

Carnegie Museum of Natural History, Pittsburgh: *Apatosaurus, Diplodocus*

Denver Museum of Natural History: *Diplodocus*

Field Museum of Natural History, Chicago: *Brachiosaurus, Diplodocus*

Houston Museum of Natural History: *Diplodocus*

National Museum of Natural History, Washington, D.C.: *Diplodocus*

New Mexico Museum of Natural History, Albuquerque: *Seismosaurus*

Peabody Museum of Natural History, New Haven, Connecticut: *Apatosaurus*

Utah Museum of Natural History, Salt Lake City: *Barosaurus*

To Erica and Rebecca, my favorite dinosaur haters — D.L.

ACKNOWLEDGMENTS

Many thanks to Professor Rodolfo Coria for his patient and expert attention to this book. Special thanks also go to Dr. Donald Baird, Kenneth Carpenter, Dr. Philip Currie, Dr. Peter Dodson, Dr. David Gillette, Thom Holmes, Jim Jensen, Dr. John McIntosh, Dr. Wade Miller, Gregory Paul, and Cliff Stadtman for their expertise and kind assistance.

ABOUT THE AUTHOR

"Dino" Don Lessem digs dinosaurs. He is the founder of the international nonprofit Dinosaur Society and its children's newspaper *Dino Times,* as well as the dinosaur columnist for *Highlights for Children* magazine. Mr. Lessem has written and hosted *Nova* documentaries and was an adviser to the film *Jurassic Park.* He is a consultant to television series, amusement parks, and museums and is the creator of exhibits and CD-ROMs. His most recent children's books are *Raptors!; Bigger than T. rex; Utahraptor: The Nastiest Dinosaur;* and *Seismosaurus: The Longest Dinosaur.* When not at home in Boston with his family, Mr. Lessem participates in dinosaur expeditions to Mongolia, Argentina, Montana, and Arctic Alaska.

ABOUT THE ILLUSTRATOR

Artist David Peters made a splash in the world of children's books with the publication of his first title, *Giants of Land, Sea & Air—Past & Present.* Mr. Peters has since written and illustrated several other books for children, including *Strange Creatures* and *From the Beginning: The Story of Human Evolution.* After shifting his focus for several years from painting to sculpture, Mr. Peters returned to children's books with *Raptors! The Nastiest Dinosaurs,* which was also written by Mr. Lessem. Mr. Peters makes his home in St. Louis.

Library of Congress Cataloging-in-Publication Data
Lessem, Don.
   Supergiants! : the biggest dinosaurs / by Don Lessem ; illustrated by David Peters ; scientific adviser, Rodolfo Coria. — 1st ed.
     p. cm.
   Summary: Describes some of the largest specimens of dinosaurs and how they were found and studied.
   ISBN 0-316-52118-3
   1. Dinosaurs — Juvenile literature. [1. Dinosaurs. 2. Fossils. 3. Paleontology.] I. Peters, David ill. II. Title.
QE862.D5L517 1997
567.9'1 — dc20   96-15418

10 9 8 7 6 5 4 3 2 1

SC

Published simultaneously in Canada by Little, Brown & Company (Canada) Limited

Printed in Hong Kong

Paintings done in acrylics on Strathmore Bristol paper

Photography Credits
Pages 8 and 9: Courtesy of the Peabody Museum of Natural History, Yale University. Page 14: Negative #229511 (photo by Julius Kirchner, 1918) Courtesy Department of Library Services, American Museum of Natural History. Pages 27–29: Courtesy of Ignacio Salas-Humara.

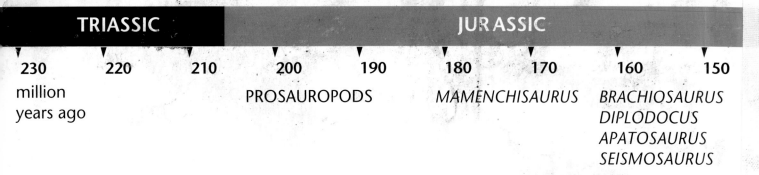

TRIASSIC

JURASSIC

230
million
years ago

220

210

200
PROSAUROPODS

190

180
MAMENCHISAURUS

170

160
BRACHIOSAURUS
DIPLODOCUS
APATOSAURUS
SEISMOSAURUS

150

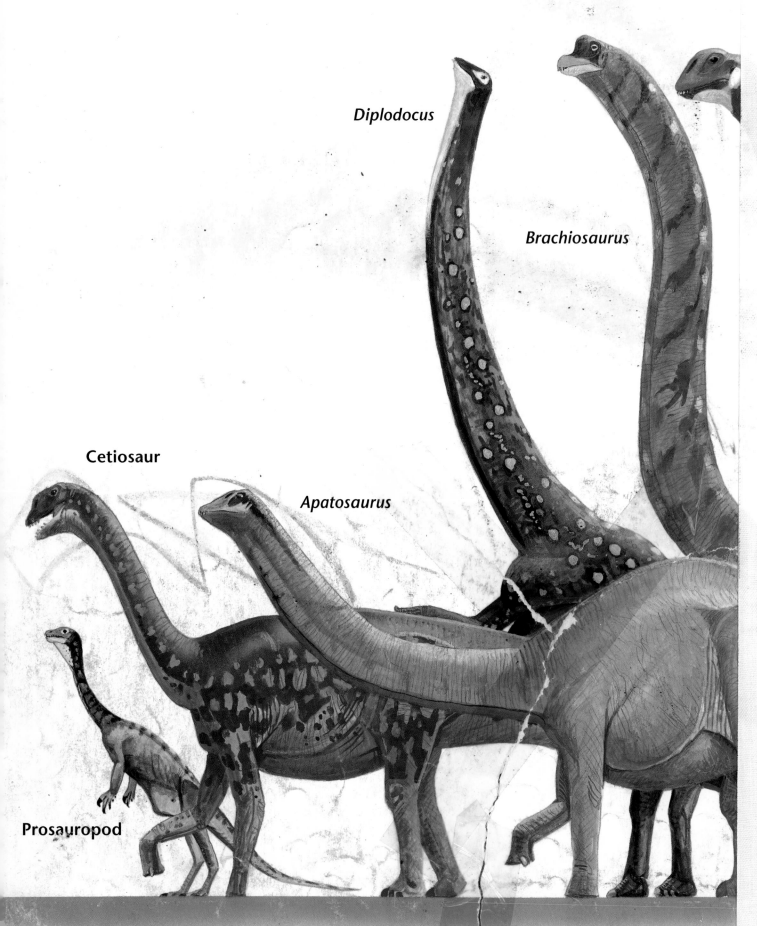

Diplodocus

Brachiosaurus

Cetiosaur

Apatosaurus

Prosauropod